BEE BRAVE
Like
KAISA
AF427486

DEDICATION:

TO KAISA MORGAN

OF MALAMA-KI HONEY BEES IN PAHOA, HAWAII,

THIS BOOK IS DEDICATED TO YOU, OUR FEARLESS FRIEND AND DEVOTED BEEKEEPER. YOUR PASSION FOR BEES AND UNWAVERING DEDICATION TO THEIR WELL-BEING INSPIRE US EVERY DAY. MAY YOUR LOVE FOR NATURE AND ALL ITS CREATURES CONTINUE TO SHINE BRIGHTLY, JUST LIKE THE GOLDEN HONEY YOUR BEES PRODUCE.

WITH GRATITUDE AND ADMIRATION,
MARCY SCHAAF
BOOKS BY SCHAAF

INTRODUCTION:

WELCOME, CURIOUS READERS, TO THE ENCHANTING WORLD OF KAISA THE BEEKEEPER! IN THIS DELIGHTFUL TALE, WE EMBARK ON A JOURNEY TO THE LUSH LANDSCAPES OF PAHOA, HAWAII, WHERE ONE REMARKABLE GIRL SHOWS US THAT WITH COURAGE AND DETERMINATION, ANYONE CAN PURSUE THEIR DREAMS – EVEN IF THOSE DREAMS INVOLVE BUZZING BEES AND SWEET HONEY.

THROUGH THE PAGES OF THIS BOOK, WE'LL JOIN KAISA AS SHE TENDS TO HER BELOVED HIVES, LEARNING IMPORTANT LESSONS ABOUT TEAMWORK, THE WONDERS OF NATURE, AND THE INCREDIBLE BOND BETWEEN HUMANS AND BEES. ALONG THE WAY, WE'LL DISCOVER THE VITAL ROLE BEES PLAY IN OUR FOOD SUPPLY, THE FASCINATING DYNAMICS OF A BEE COLONY, AND THE HEARTWARMING WAYS THESE TINY CREATURES CAN LEND A HELPING WING WHEN WE NEED IT MOST.

SO, DEAR READERS, PREPARE TO BE SWEPT AWAY BY THE MAGIC OF KAISA'S WORLD, WHERE EVERY FLOWER HOLDS A SECRET, EVERY BEE HAS A STORY, AND EVERY STING IS A GENTLE REMINDER OF THE POWER OF FRIENDSHIP AND HEALING. LET'S OPEN OUR HEARTS AND MINDS TO THE BUZZING ADVENTURES THAT AWAIT US IN THE PAGES AHEAD. ARE YOU READY? LET'S DIVE IN AND EXPLORE THE BUZZING WONDERS OF KAISA THE BEEKEEPER!

MEET KAISA,
THE FEARLESS BEEKEEPER OF
PAHOA, HAWAII!

KAISA LOVED BEES. SHE WORE A
WIDE-BRIMMED HAT AND A GENTLE
SMILE AS SHE TENDED TO HER HIVES.

SOME PEOPLE SAID, "BEEKEEPING IS FOR BOYS."
BUT KAISA KNEW BETTER.

SHE'D WHISPER TO HER BUZZING FRIENDS, "GIRLS CAN DO ANY JOB THEY DREAM!"

WITH DETERMINATION IN HER HEART, KAISA SHOWED
THE WORLD THAT BEEKEEPING WAS HER PASSION.

IN HER GARDEN, FLOWERS DANCED HAPPILY,
THANKS TO HER BUSY BEE FRIENDS.

BEES ARE LIKE NATURE'S SUPERHEROES, ESSENTIAL FOR OUR FOOD TO GROW BIG AND STRONG.

THEY FLY FROM FLOWER TO FLOWER,
SPREADING POLLEN, SO FRUITS AND VEGGIES
CAN BLOSSOM.

IN THE HIVE, EACH BEE HAS A SPECIAL ROLE: THE QUEEN, THE NURSE, THE GUARD, AND MORE.

THE QUEEN LAYS EGGS, THE NURSE CARES FOR BABIES, AND THE GUARD PROTECTS THE HIVE.

SOME BEES ARE BUILDERS, CRAFTING INTRICATE HONEYCOMBS WITH MATHEMATICAL PRECISION.

TOGETHER, THEY CREATE A BUZZING SYMPHONY OF TEAMWORK

ENSURING THE SURVIVAL OF THEIR COLONY.

JUST LIKE IN THE HIVE, EVERY
PERSON HAS UNIQUE TALENTS.
THEY MAKE THE WORLD A BETTER
PLACE, TOO.

WITHOUT BEES, OUR PLATES WOULD BE EMPTY, AND OUR WORLD A LITTLE LESS SWEET.
GOLDEN HONEY!

SO LET'S GIVE A CHEER FOR OUR TINY, BUZZING FRIENDS WHO KEEP OUR FOOD SUPPLY THRIVING!

ARE YOU AFRAID OF BEES?

ONE DAY, KAISA ACCIDENTALLY TRIPPED
OVER A ROCK AND SCRAPED HER KNEE.

BUT BEFORE SHE COULD EVEN BLINK, HER
LOYAL BEES FLEW TO HER RESCUE.

WITH GENTLE PRECISION, THEY LANDED
ON HER WOUND, GIVING HER TINY
STINGS FILLED WITH HEALING MEDICINE.

AS THE PAIN MELTED AWAY,
KAISA SMILED, KNOWING HER BEE
FRIENDS HAD HER BACK.

YOU SEE, BEES AREN'T JUST ABOUT HONEY –
THEY'RE NATURE'S NURSES, TOO!

SO NEXT TIME YOU SEE A BEE BUZZING BY,
REMEMBER, THEY'RE HERE TO HELP, NOT TO HARM.

WITH A GRATEFUL HEART, KAISA THANKED
HER BUZZING BUDDIES FOR THEIR
KINDNESS.

AS THE SUN DIPPED LOW, KAISA SAT BY HER HIVES, LISTENING
TO THE GENTLE HUM OF HER FUZZY FRIENDS.

REMEMBER, NO JOB IS OFF-LIMITS TO YOU, WHETHER IT'S BEEKEEPING OR REACHING FOR THE STARS!

MAHALO, MY DEAR FRIENDS.
THE END

IF YOU'RE EVER ON THE BIG ISLAND OF HAWAII STOP BY THE MAKU'U FARMERS MARKET ON SUNDAY AND MEET KAISA!

THE REAL KAISA MORGAN
MALAMA-KI HONEY BEES

PROJECT: DIY BEESWAX FOOD WRAPS

MATERIALS NEEDED:
- COTTON FABRIC (PREFERABLY LIGHTWEIGHT AND BREATHABLE)
- BEESWAX PELLETS OR GRATED BEESWAX
- PINE RESIN (OPTIONAL, FOR ADDED STICKINESS)
- JOJOBA OIL OR COCONUT OIL (OPTIONAL, FOR FLEXIBILITY)
- PARCHMENT PAPER
- BAKING SHEET
- CLOTHESLINE OR DRYING RACK

INSTRUCTIONS:

1. START BY CUTTING YOUR COTTON FABRIC INTO SQUARES OR RECTANGLES OF VARIOUS SIZES, DEPENDING ON YOUR PREFERENCE AND THE CONTAINERS YOU PLAN TO COVER.

2. PREHEAT YOUR OVEN TO 200°F (93°C) AND LINE A BAKING SHEET WITH PARCHMENT PAPER.

3. PLACE ONE PIECE OF FABRIC ON THE PARCHMENT PAPER-LINED BAKING SHEET.

4. SPRINKLE A GENEROUS AMOUNT OF BEESWAX PELLETS OR GRATED BEESWAX EVENLY OVER THE FABRIC. IF DESIRED, YOU CAN ALSO ADD A SMALL AMOUNT OF PINE RESIN FOR EXTRA STICKINESS AND JOJOBA OIL OR COCONUT OIL FOR FLEXIBILITY.

5. PLACE ANOTHER PIECE OF PARCHMENT PAPER ON TOP OF THE FABRIC AND BEESWAX TO CREATE A SANDWICH.

6. PLACE THE BAKING SHEET IN THE PREHEATED OVEN AND ALLOW THE BEESWAX TO MELT ONTO THE FABRIC. THIS SHOULD TAKE ABOUT 5-10 MINUTES, DEPENDING ON THE THICKNESS OF THE FABRIC AND THE AMOUNT OF BEESWAX USED.

7. CAREFULLY REMOVE THE BAKING SHEET FROM THE OVEN ONCE THE BEESWAX HAS MELTED COMPLETELY. USE A PAINTBRUSH OR SPATULA TO SPREAD THE MELTED BEESWAX EVENLY OVER THE FABRIC, ENSURING THAT EVERY INCH IS COVERED.

8. LIFT THE TOP LAYER OF PARCHMENT PAPER AND CHECK IF THERE ARE ANY DRY SPOTS ON THE FABRIC. IF SO, SPRINKLE A LITTLE MORE BEESWAX OVER THOSE AREAS AND RETURN THE BAKING SHEET TO THE OVEN FOR A FEW MORE MINUTES UNTIL FULLY MELTED.

9. ONCE THE FABRIC IS EVENLY COATED WITH BEESWAX, CAREFULLY LIFT IT OFF THE PARCHMENT PAPER AND HANG IT ON A CLOTHESLINE OR DRYING RACK TO COOL AND HARDEN.

10. REPEAT THE PROCESS WITH THE REMAINING PIECES OF FABRIC UNTIL YOU'VE MADE AS MANY BEESWAX WRAPS AS YOU LIKE.

11. ONCE COOLED AND HARDENED, YOUR DIY BEESWAX FOOD WRAPS ARE READY TO USE! SIMPLY USE THE WARMTH OF YOUR HANDS TO MOLD THE WRAPS AROUND FOOD CONTAINERS, BOWLS, OR DIRECTLY OVER FOOD ITEMS TO CREATE A SEAL. THE BEESWAX WILL STICK TO ITSELF AND HOLD ITS SHAPE, CREATING A NATURAL ALTERNATIVE TO PLASTIC WRAP THAT'S REUSABLE AND ECO-FRIENDLY.

ENJOY USING YOUR HOMEMADE BEESWAX WRAPS TO KEEP YOUR FOOD FRESH AND REDUCE YOUR PLASTIC WASTE!

Books By Schaaf

www.BookBySchaaf.com

Find us at: